The Entertaining Groom

The Entertaining Groom

Stewart Mair and Iain Mair

Contents

Why We Wrote This Book

Your wedding is one of the biggest days of your life. We wrote this book to ensure that, as the groom, you have the best possible experience and that your special day lives up to your greatest expectations. To that end, we wanted both to highlight the main responsibilities that come with being a groom, and also help you write and deliver a brilliant, entertaining and witty speech.

Most of the responsibilities that come with being a groom, which are listed below, are fairly straightforward. On the other hand, unless you're a professional public speaker or a natural extrovert, you're likely to find duty no. 15 below—giving the groom's speech at the reception—more than a little daunting (if not terrifying).

Unfortunately there's nothing we can do to help you with stage fright, except extend our condolences. However, what we can do is provide a framework to guide you in the creation of your speech. Based on our own experience as grooms, and as guests at many weddings, we believe that humor is an essential part of the groom's speech and, accordingly we have included some of the best jokes available. We hope that this framework will help you deal with any dread you may be feeling and that it may even make the process of writing and delivering your speech an enjoyable one.

There is a mountain of information out there on being a groom. Our goal was to create a single, concise book that clearly summarizes the key responsibilities involved, and also contains a great selection of jokes that will entertain your audience. If you use our template to structure your speech, add significant personal events, and include the jokes that you feel will best appeal to the attendees, you'll succeed brilliantly.

GROOM'S DUTIES

1. Help decide the budget for the wedding, in consultation with any parents who are paying or contributing.
2. Buy the wedding rings.
3. Help choose the date, style and location for the wedding and arrange reservations and any deposits.
4. Help coordinate the invitations, flowers, photographer, etc.
5. Meet with the person who will be performing the ceremony.
6. Attend the bachelor party, which is usually organized by the best man.
7. Help to organize the wedding attire for yourself and your groomsmen.
8. Plan and pay for the honeymoon.
9. Obtain the marriage license.
10. Purchase gifts for the wedding party (best man, ushers and bridesmaids).
11. Purchase a wedding gift for your wife.
12. On the wedding day, support your bride wherever you can.
13. Liaise with the wedding party to ensure that everything is progressing smoothly.

14. Make sure the photographer has taken all of the photographs you want.
15. Give the groom's speech at the reception (see below for typical order of speeches).
16. Dance with your bride at the reception.
17. Help to write the thank you notes for the wedding gifts.

SPEECH-WRITING TIPS

1. Start working on your speech at least one month before the wedding (we would recommend even earlier). Begin by writing down all of the ideas that come into your head. Don't worry at this point if they seem silly or inappropriate—you can always decide not to use them later. In addition, ask family and friends for any relevant stories that can be included. It is also recommended that you consult your wife regarding the content and tone of the speech.

2. When you've collected all the information, choose the ideas and stories you like best and insert them in the appropriate sections of the framework we've provided below.

3. Be tactful and sensitive, and try not to lie.

4. Once everything is in place, review the speech in its totality and make any modifications that seem desirable.

5. Leave the speech for a couple of days, and then come back and make further modifications. Keep doing this until you are happy with it.

6. Once the speech is finalized, practice reading it out loud. Read it again and again until the words start becoming familiar.

7. We would also recommend reading it in front of one or more people, such as a friend or family member.

SPEECH DELIVERY

1. If you are not accustomed to making speeches, bring a printed copy to the wedding so you can refer to it if needed. Alternatively, you can use cards that contain key components of the speech to help ensure that you don't lose your place.

2. Try not to be nervous. Everyone in the room will be supporting you. When it's your turn, be sure to stand up with a smile on your face.

3. Relax and take your time.

4. If you start to feel that you're going on too long, don't be afraid to cut some things out.

5. Do not swear.

6. Be yourself.

7. Try not to drink too much before you speak.

8. Give it your best effort and try to enjoy the experience.

ORDER OF SPEECHES

Since guests are usually hungry after the wedding ceremony, the speeches normally come after the meal. The order is traditionally as follows:

1. If there is a Master of Ceremonies, he or she will speak first and introduce the speakers.

2. *Father of the Bride:* Welcomes guests and mentions those who could not make it and those who have travelled a long way. He will then talk fondly about his daughter and congratulate the groom on his choice of a wife. He will also talk about meeting the groom's family and might tell some stories about preparing for the wedding. The speech ends with a toast to the bride and groom.

3. *Groom:* The groom thanks his wife's father for welcoming him into the family and for the privilege of marrying his daughter. He will thank his parents for their support and guidance and thank the people who helped with the wedding preparations. He'll also thank the guests for attending and for their gifts, and extend thanks to the best man and groomsmen for their support. He will then talk about his wife before proposing a toast to the bridesmaids.

4. *Best Man:* The best man thanks the bride and
   groom on behalf of the bridesmaids and himself
   for asking them to be part of their special day, and
   congratulates the bride and groom on their union.
   He then goes on to talk about the groom and his
   relationship with him. This is usually the high
   point in the speeches. Finally, he reads telegrams,
   cards, e-mails or other messages from friends and
   relatives who could not attend. It should be noted
   that the best man is not responsible for toasting the
   bride and groom.

GROOM'S SPEECH FRAMEWORK

We have provided a broad selection of jokes and other speech components for you to choose from. Select the material that is most appropriate and that will work best for your wedding.

While the focus here is on making the speech entertaining, it is also extremely important that it revolves around your bride in a highly complementary way, and reflect the seriousness and joy of the occasion.

Welcome

Distinguished guests, family, friends and [NAME OF A WELL-KNOWN GUEST / CHARACTER]. On behalf of my wife [BRIDE'S NAME] and I, we would like to thank everyone for coming today and we are delighted to see you.

Ladies and gentlemen, I'd like to thank all of you for being here today, especially those of you who knew that I'd be saying a few words and decided to come anyway.

Welcome, ladies and gentlemen. On behalf of my wife and I, we would like to thank you all for coming. Having you all here means so much to us and we are glad you can be here to celebrate our special day.

Good evening, ladies and gentlemen. Before I get into my speech, [BRIDE'S NAME] has just asked me to clarify that when she cried during the ceremony, those were tears of joy. In case anyone was wondering.

Distinguished guests, guests of no particular distinction, relatives young and old, friends, freeloaders, hangers-on, gate-crashers, and anyone else who may have wandered in. We would like to thank everyone for coming today and we are delighted to see you.

Hello, ladies and gentlemen. It's lovely to see so many of our family and friends here today to help us celebrate the happiest day of our lives. It really wouldn't be the same without you all. It might be a little cheaper, but not the same.

We would like to welcome everyone here today. The fact that you are in this room means that we care about you a lot. So, congratulations, you made the cut.

Welcome, ladies and gentlemen, and thanks for joining us to celebrate the happiest day of our lives. I don't want to take up too much of your drinking time, so I'll keep this brief.

Good evening, ladies and gentlemen. I have been told that this is one of the only times in a married man's life when he can be in the company of his wife and mother in-law and not be interrupted. Therefore, I may be here for some time.

We would like to thank everyone for coming today. It just wouldn't be the same if it were just me and [BRIDE'S NAME].

I did try to memorize my speech, but I have a memory like a geriatric goldfish, so I'll be reading from my notes here. [THIS IS USEFUL IF ARE PLANNING ON READING YOUR NOTES DIRECTLY].

I have to confess I've been terrified about giving this speech, although maybe not quite as terrified as [BRIDE'S NAME].

I am under strict instructions not to have a drink until after the first toast. So you'll have to excuse me if I seem in a hurry to finish.

Now, I'm not going to stand up here and bore you with bad jokes. I'll leave that to the best man.

I'm not an experienced public speaker, so I find it easier just to read the speech word for word. In fact, I've been practicing it daily for about a week-and-a half now, which is a tip that I picked up in a book about public speaking. I've also been drinking profusely for the last two hours. I made that tip up myself.

I've really sweated and suffered over this speech and now it's your turn.

I just want to let you know that, to help my nervousness, I am picturing all of you in your underwear. It's not a pretty sight.

I have to admit I'm very nervous about making this speech. To put my nervousness in perspective, this is the fifth time this afternoon that I've risen from a warm seat with a piece of paper in my hand.

I have to admit that I'm very nervous about making this speech. In fact, it reminds me of a story about the famous British admiral, Lord Nelson. He was asked why he always put on a red tunic before a battle. He said it was so the enemy wouldn't see the blood if he got injured. So, ladies and gentlemen, this explains why I am wearing brown underpants tonight.

I am a little nervous about making this speech. The last time I had to speak in public was at Alcoholics Anonymous. But I have to say, it's nice to see so many familiar faces here today.

Now, as is the custom, there will be a few toasts during my speech. So please don't drink your whole glass at the first toast . . . mentioning no names, mom.

I stand here before you as a different man. I am a married man. But, in many ways, nothing much has changed. I can sit and watch TV all day, make my own decisions, eat what I like and drink what I like—isn't that right, dear?

A wise man once said that a speech should last as long as the groom can make love—I would make sure you have your glasses topped up, as it could be a long night.

Now I'd like to lay down a couple of ground rules. First, no heckling, please. Second, I've been asked to remind you that, for health and safety reasons, no one is to get up on the tables and chairs during my standing ovation.

In preparation for this speech, I was reminded about the ABC & XYZ of public speaking. ABC— Always Be Confident. Hopefully, that won't be a problem. And XYZ— Examine Your Zipper! [TURN AROUND AND CHECK YOUR ZIPPER BEFORE GIVING A THUMBS UP]

This speech is going to have so many thank yous that you'll think you're at the Oscars. After hearing it, you will soon realize that you aren't.

Ladies and gentlemen, I have to say I just can't wait to get back and get those knickers off tonight. I've been looking forward to it all day. That's right, I bought a new pair for the wedding and they've been itching like crazy all day.

We would like to say a special thanks to those people who have traveled a long way to be here.

I better get started because my wife said if I don't keep the speech short, she's going to cut it.

Gifts

We would like to thank you all for your generosity and the fantastic gifts you have given us.

We'd like to thank all of you for your generous gifts and we really appreciate your kindness.

I can't tell you how much the gifts mean to us. I will however have a better idea after the honeymoon when I've had chance to list them on eBay.

As you can imagine, with so many people attending the wedding, it created a bit of an issue with the seating plan and deciding who should sit where. So, in the end, we decided to use the gift list as a guide. Those who gave the best presents are sitting in the front and those who weren't so generous are sitting in back. So, I think they've had enough wine in the back now.

Mother & Father-In-Law

I'd like to thank [FATHER-IN-LAW'S NAME] for his kind words and best wishes.

I'd like to thank [FATHER-IN-LAW'S NAME] for his speech. I knew it would be hard to follow and I was right. I could hardly follow a word of it.

Thank you, [FATHER-IN-LAW'S NAME], for those kind words. I imagine it must have been hard giving away your daughter today. Although, when you escorted [BRIDE'S NAME] down the aisle I could have sworn I saw you running.

I'd like to thank [FATHER-IN-LAW'S NAME] for his kind words and introduction just now. (TO FATHER-IN-LAW) [FATHER-IN-LAW'S NAME], you can be my warm-up act anytime.

I would like to thank [FATHER-IN-LAW'S NAME] for his kind words. I hope that, as [BRIDE'S NAME] husband, I can live up to the great image he painted of me there. Or, if not, at least keep pulling the wool over his eyes.

I'd like to thank [FATHER-IN-LAW'S NAME] for giving away [BRIDE'S NAME] this morning so willingly. I was a little bit surprised at how willingly he gave her away.

Having spoken to [FATHER-IN-LAW'S NAME], I know he always had such high hopes for [BRIDE'S NAME]. Well, I guess that's all come to an end now.

I would like to say a big thank you to [FATHER-IN-LAW'S NAME] and [MOTHER-IN-LAW'S NAME] and the rest of the [FAMILY LAST NAME]s for making me feel like a part of the family from day one. I've never had the chance to say thank you properly—so thank you.

And now moving on to [BRIDE'S NAME]'s parents, [FATHER-IN-LAW'S NAME] and [MOTHER-IN-LAW'S NAME]. Traditionally I am supposed to thank you both at this point for welcoming

27

me into your family, but it seems strange for me to do that today as you have both made me feel like a part of it for many years now.

I have to thank both [FATHER-IN-LAW'S NAME] and [MOTHER-IN-LAW'S NAME] for bringing up such a beautiful and intelligent daughter. I'll leave you to argue over which trait comes from whom.

I would like to thank you for the gift of your beautiful, intelligent and amazing daughter. I'm looking forward to unwrapping her later tonight.

Now, it's commonly said that if you want to know what your wife will look like in years to come, look to the mother. Well, I'm looking and I'm liking. [BRIDE'S NAME], on the other hand, if you look towards my father—things are not looking so promising for you.

Being a staunch traditionalist, I did the time-honored, decent thing when it came to proposing to [BRIDE'S NAME]. I went down on one knee . . . and then went down on the other . . . and I asked her father if he would pay for the wedding.

I would like to thank [BRIDE'S NAME]'s parents for bringing up such an amazing and wonderful daughter. Why you didn't teach her to iron and cook, I'm not quite sure.

Now I know [FATHER-IN-LAW'S NAME] trusts me with his daughter, as he's already given me a receipt to sign. It reads:

"Received, one daughter in perfect condition, fully guaranteed and warranted. Keep topped up with expensive jewelry, foreign trips and shoes, and lubricate with vintage wine. Comes complete with all extras."

Not to be outdone, my father has a receipt for [BRIDE'S NAME] to sign. It reads:

"Received, one son. Sold as is, no refunds under any circumstances. Dehydrates easily, top up regularly with beer."

I must say, it's funny how history repeats itself. [XX] years ago, [BRIDE'S NAME]'s mum and dad were sending their daughter to bed with a dummy—and here we are again today.

[BRIDE'S NAME] is in good hands now and I promise to do my best to ensure that she looks after me properly.

Parents

I would also like to thank my parents because . . . quite frankly, I wouldn't be here without them.

30

Mom and dad. Give yourself a pat on the back. Haven't you done well.

Thank you for producing such an incredible son. I know you can't believe how fortunate you are to have me. But as we all know, today is not about me, but [BRIDE'S NAME].

I would like to say thank you to my parents for producing such an incredible, stunningly handsome son. You have been a great help to me over the years and seen me through thick and thin. Mostly thick. But I thank you for everything that you've done, and not just for me, but for me and [BRIDE'S NAME].

I would like to thank my parents for their help and support over the years. You should be proud that you raised an intelligent, witty, dashing, handsome son, but unfortunately, you raised me. So thanks for putting up with me and being here today to support [BRIDE'S NAME] and me.

I would like to thank mom and dad for their support over the years and for making me into the sex god you see today.

I would like to thank my parents for everything they have done in my life, and I am sorry for everything I have done to theirs.

I feel that I cannot let this occasion pass without mentioning what a wonderful example my mom and dad have set for me. Besides their loving devotion as parents, they have demonstrated an unfailing devotion to each other. The least I can do is follow their lead.

BRIDE

The groom should add comments about how he and his wife met and how the relationship developed. Also, include an amusing story about something that happened during the wedding preparations.

Now to my wife, and I can't even begin to tell you how absolutely, stunningly gorgeous you look today.

And now, moving on to the star of today, my gorgeous new wife [BRIDE'S NAME] – I can't even begin to tell you how absolutely, stunningly gorgeous you look today.

When I saw you coming up the aisle, I realized how lucky I am—and it's definitely me that's getting the best part of this deal. You are caring, funny, and intelligent and I'm looking forward to spending the rest of my life with you.

We are told that marriage is a lottery. Well, if it is, then I've hit the jackpot.

They say you don't marry someone you can live with; you marry the person you can't live without.

Tradition dictates that I now tell you an amusing story or two about how [BRIDE'S NAME] and I met. Unfortunately [BRIDE'S NAME] dictates that I do no such thing.

I remember the first time I met [BRIDE'S NAME] and thinking, why can't I get a girl like that? And now I have. You have to be very careful what you wish for.

[IF YOU ARE CHUBBY] Personally I think [BRIDE'S NAME] has a thing for chubby men. And looking around the room today, I've never seen so much competition.

Now, as you know, one of us in this relationship is a little big-headed, stubborn, and always giving advice, from how to act in the bedroom to how to cut the lawn. Luckily for me, [BRIDE'S NAME] has been patient, open-minded and willing to learn.

The first night I went out with my wife, she got me drunk and seduced me. It was then I knew she was the person for me.

I will always remember the first time I met [BRIDE'S NAME], because it was quite early in the evening and I hadn't been drinking too much.

When it comes to my bride's good points, where do I start? She's intelligent, generous, hardworking, popular—and, most of all, a brilliant judge of character.

We've been planning this wedding for some months now and I never knew it would be such hard work. And luckily for me, it wasn't. I'd like to say a big thanks to [BRIDE'S NAME] for her amazing organizational skills and hard work.

We've been planning this wedding for some months now. Well, I say "we," but really [BRIDE'S NAME] did all the work. I just agreed to take care of the weather. [IF IT'S NICE] And I don't think I've done too badly. [IF IT'S NOT NICE] And I even screwed that up.

One thing I would like to say is, having now been through it all, I can't understand why people say arranging a wedding is such a stressful business. From what I could see, most if it seems to have just taken care of itself.

Wedding organizing hasn't really been an equal-opportunity thing, but my wife did let me sign all of the checks.

In our house, we have wedding magazines, to-do lists and papers everywhere. In fact, I woke up the other day with a sticky note on my forehead that said, "Don't forget to bring to the wedding."

It has been a real team effort preparing for this wedding. My wife organized the hotel, cars, flowers, dresses and the cake, while I was thinking about writing my speech. Then my wife issued the invitations, did the seating plan and planned the ceremony, while I started working on my speech. And this week, my wife made sure that all the finishing touches were complete and everything was in its place, while I did the finishing touches on my speech. It's been a real team effort.

I am so lucky to have [BRIDE'S NAME], but a while ago I started having nightmares that [BRIDE'S NAME] had left me. Although, it was a great feeling when I woke up next to her to realize that she was still there. I knew she was the one for me and promptly proposed. My nightmares ended and [BRIDE'S NAME]'s dreams came true.

For those of you who know [BRIDE'S NAME], she is a bit of a fitness freak. The house has been like a boot camp over the last couple of months—detoxing, dieting, diet pills, diet shakes, protein shakes, personal trainers, nutritionists, yoga, running, cycling. And [BRIDE'S NAME] also managed to fit in a couple of exercises as well.

I was telling [BRIDE'S NAME] that no wife of mine is going to work. All she'll need to do is the washing, ironing, cooking, cleaning and shopping.

My wife is wonderful and only ever has two complaints. Number one, she has nothing to wear, and number two, there's never enough space in her closet.

I do love the fact that [BRIDE'S NAME] puts up with all of my faults. Maybe not always in silence.

I was reading a book recently about being the man of the house and I was telling my wife that, as the man of the house, my word is law. Therefore, I want a gourmet meal on the table every night followed by a lovely dessert. After the dishes have been cleaned up, I want to have a nice hot bath run for me so I can relax after a hard day's work. And then, when I come out of the bath, guess who's going to dress me and comb my hair? And she said, "My guess would be the funeral director."

My wife hinted for a long time about wanting to get married. Whenever I bought her flowers, she turned around and threw them back over her head.

I have to say that [BRIDE'S NAME] has always been there in times of trouble. Usually screaming, "You caused this, you idiot!"

One thing I have learnt is to always hold [BRIDE'S NAME]'s hand when we go out. If I don't, she shops.

[BRIDE'S NAME] is a great cook and the last meal she made was lovely. It was a little burnt, but a lovely salad none the less.

Many of you know it took us a while to get to where we are today. The traffic on [NAME OF LOCAL HIGHWAY] was a nightmare.

[BRIDE'S NAME] does sometimes says that I never listen to her. At least I think that's what she said.

I always refer to [BRIDE'S NAME] as an angel. That's because she's always flying around the house harping about something.

When [BRIDE'S NAME] finally agreed to go out with me, I tried to impress her by taking her out to a really fancy restaurant. And the evening went very well. I made her laugh so hard that she dropped her fries.

I think we complement each other very well. [BRIDE'S NAME] is ambitious, highly motivated and loves a challenge. And I am that challenge.

[BRIDE'S NAME] and I are very well suited to each other. I am the boss in the relationship, while [BRIDE'S NAME] is just the decision-maker.

I think you'll agree that [BRIDE'S NAME] looks stunning in that magnificent white dress. I feel so proud and honored to be married to her. And of course, I can at last say, my dishwasher matches my fridge.

I can't believe that such a wonderful woman chose to marry me. I love you very much and I'm looking forward to the many years to come.

Ushers

I'd like to thank the ushers today. They've done a great job of "ushing," which has not been an easy job with the crowd we've had here today.

The only request we made of the ushers was that they look good. And, they let us down somewhat there.

Wedding etiquette states that no one should look better than the groom. I'd like to thank the ushers for abiding by the rules.

We call [USHER'S NAME] the exorcist in our house. Every time he comes by, he disposes of all our spirits.

A number of us have been pointing out to [USHER'S NAME] that it's about time he settles down himself. They say marriage is a matter of give and take. So far he hasn't been able to find anybody who will take what he has to give.

I heard a rumor that [USHER'S NAME] made the mistake of asking [MOTHER-IN-LAW'S NAME] on the way in to the service, "Excuse me, are you a friend of the groom's?" And she said, "Certainly not – I'm the bride's mother!"

Best Man

I'd like to thank [BEST MAN'S NAME] for being my best man.

It was important to me to have a best man with morals and principles. Sadly, he couldn't make it, so I ended up with

[BEST MAN'S NAME]. I believe he'll be demonstrating this in his speech.

A best man is someone who is organized, caring and thoughtful. I'm still searching for this person, but at the moment I have [BEST MAN'S NAME].

And now, moving on to the best man, [BEST MAN'S NAME]. Every now and again, we get the opportunity to talk about a man of the highest integrity and honor. A man of achievement and action, who is obviously destined for great things. Unfortunately, ladies and gentlemen, that is not going to happen just now.

As for my best man, I couldn't ask for a finer one, and I wish you all the best with your speech. If you feel a little nervous, just remember everyone is watching.

To my best man, you are a true friend and I am delighted to have you as best man. You are a really great guy who would never make fun of me in public. So, I wish you all the best with your speech.

Now, I'm not going to embarrass [BEST MAN'S NAME] too much. Because we all know he's quite capable of doing that himself.

The other day, I was asking [BEST MAN'S NAME]'s father [BEST MAN'S FATHER'S NAME] about [BEST MAN'S NAME], and he was recalling him as a baby—hairy, plump and always wanting to be the center of attention. Come to think of it, he hasn't changed a bit.

I can honestly say, in all the years I've known [BEST MAN'S NAME], no one has ever questioned his intelligence. In fact, I've never heard anyone even mention it.

[BEST MAN'S NAME] has a reputation for being a six-times-a-night man. He's always had a weak bladder.

We have a best man who knows a great deal about love. Although, most of his is aimed at the mirror.

When [BEST MAN'S NAME] was 13, his dad told him to think before he speaks. No one heard a word from him for two months.

[IF YOUR BROTHER IS THE BEST MAN] I feel like I have known my best man all my life. He's really been like a brother to me. I have to imagine it must have been hard for [BEST MAN'S NAME], having to follow my lead when he was growing up.

I found it hard to pick a best man, since I've made a lot of great friends over the years—friends who are always there for me through thick and thin. It's a shame none of them could make it today, so I'm making do with [BEST MAN'S NAME].

It's only right that I advise you all before his speech—he's a true friend and I wouldn't want you to upset him. So if you could bear with him, and join him on his journey of make-believe, I would appreciate it.

I would like to thank [BEST MAN'S NAME] for organizing the bachelor party, and thanks to everyone who attended. I've been told I had a good time.

Service

I'd like to thank [NAME OF PERSON WHO PERFORMED THE SERVICE] for the service. Over the past few weeks, he/she has been meeting with [BRIDE'S NAME] and me to help us understand marriage in its proper religious and moral context. I have also been seeing an independent financial advisor . . . to help me understand it in its proper economic context. I don't know who's praying harder—[NAME OF PERSON WHO PERFORMED THE SERVICE] or my financial advisor.

I'd like to thank [NAME OF PERSON WHO PERFORMED THE SERVICE] for the great job he/she did today. I learned something new during the vows that I hadn't realized before—apparently it's OK to have sixteen wives . . . four better, four worse, four richer and four poorer. So I appreciate that teaching.

Thanks to [NAME OF PERSON WHO PERFORMED THE SERVICE] for conducting the service. I was asking [NAME OF PERSON WHO PERFORMED THE SERVICE] earlier if he/she believed in sex before the wedding. And he/she said, "Not if it delays the ceremony."

OTHER

Insert additional special thanks to those who have helped with the wedding preparations.

BRIDESMAIDS

There are [NUMBER] beautiful ladies here today needing our thanks: [NAME OF BRIDESMAIDS]. We'd like to thank you very much for being such wonderful bridesmaids and you have done a great job helping out with the wedding and making sure [BRIDE'S NAME] didn't run off somewhere at the last minute.

Thanks to the bridesmaids for getting [BRIDE'S NAME] to the church on time, which is a trick you'll have to teach me sometime.

I would just like to mention the bridesmaids, who I am sure you will agree look wonderful and performed their role fantastically well, despite the inevitable rivalry that can sometimes occur. In fact, just before the service, I overheard a furious argument about who was going to be first to dance with the best man. Thinking this was good news for the best man, I got a little closer, but then I realized they were saying, "You!" "No, you!"

So, if you would please be up standing and join me in a toast to the bridesmaids. To the bridesmaids.

So, a very big thank you to these terrific young ladies who really are the most beautiful in the room, next to my bride . . . and of course, my mother-in-law.

Ladies and gentlemen, a toast to the bridesmaids.

EXAMPLE GROOM'S SPEECH

Welcome

Distinguished guests, family, friends and John William McIntyre. On behalf of my wife Elizabeth and I, we would like to thank everyone for coming today and we are delighted to see you.

As you can imagine, with so many people coming from so far to be here, it created a bit of an issue with the seating plan and deciding who should sit where. So, in the end, we decided to use the gift list as a guide. Those who gave the best presents are sitting at the front and those who weren't so generous are sitting in back. So, I think they've had enough wine in the back now.

I would like to start off by thanking Ron for his kind words and best wishes. I have to say he kept me guessing for a while when I tried to get his blessing before proposing to Elizabeth. I had planned to propose on a Friday and I called Ron on the Tuesday before, but I couldn't get through. I left a message saying I would like to have a discussion with him and could he call me back. I waited until Wednesday evening and called again and left another message. Well, Thursday came and there was still no return call. I was getting a little concerned at this stage and left another slightly desperate message saying there was a very important thing I wanted to discuss with him and could he please call me back. At this stage, he would have had a pretty good idea about why I was calling. Finally, on Friday, he called me back. He claims that he was working long hours in the Western United States and it was difficult for him to call, although I'm not sure I'm 100% convinced by that. But, thankfully he gave his blessing.

I would also like to thank my dad for his kind words. I think the idea of an American coming into the family has been quite a scary prospect for him. This is someone who has left Ayrshire about three times in his life. I think it was quite a relief for him that we decided to have the wedding ceremony here in Scotland. And it's probably for the best, because I had a big enough job persuading him to go up to Glasgow to try on the kilts for the wedding.

Mother & Father-in-law

I would like to say a big thank you to Ron and Elaine and the rest of the Angoves for making me feel like a part of the family from day one. I've never had the chance to say thank you properly— so thank you. I would also like to thank you for the gift of your beautiful, intelligent—OK, sometimes a little crazy—but amazing daughter. I can tell you both that her happiness is important to me and I promise to do you proud.

Now, it's commonly said if you want to know what your wife will look like in years to come, then look to the mother. Well, I'm looking and I'm liking. Elizabeth, on the other hand, if you look right and towards the end of the table—things are not looking so promising for you.

Parents

I would also like to say thank you to my parents for producing such an incredible, stunningly handsome son. As for Alastair and Iain, I'm not quite sure what went wrong there. You have helped over the years and seen me through thick and thin. Mainly thick. But I thank you for everything that you've done, and not just for me, but for me and Elizabeth.

Bride

As for my wife, I can't even begin to tell you how absolutely, stunningly gorgeous you look today. When I saw you coming up the aisle, I realized how lucky I am, and it's definitely me that's getting the best part of this deal. I will always remember the first time I met Elizabeth in Dublin, because it was quite early in the evening and I hadn't been drinking much yet. We met at a meet-up event for new people in Dublin and quickly grew to be very close. You are caring, funny, and intelligent and I've had a great couple of years with you. I'm looking forward to spending the rest of my life with you.

We've been planning this wedding for some months now, and I never knew preparing for a wedding would be such hard work. And luckily for me, it wasn't. I'd like to say a big thanks to Elizabeth for her amazing organization skills and hard work. In our house, we have wedding magazines, to-do lists and papers everywhere. In fact, I woke up the other day with a sticky note on my forehead saying, "Don't forget to bring to the wedding."

For those of you who know Elizabeth, she is a bit of a fitness freak. The house has been like a boot camp over the last couple of months—detoxing, dieting, diet pills, diet shakes, protein shakes, personal trainers, nutritionists, yoga, running, cycling. And Elizabeth managed to fit in a couple of exercises as well.

We're planning to move to Mexico for my work shortly after we return from our honeymoon, and I was asking Elizabeth recently if she could live on my income. And she said, of course, but what are you going to live on? If any of you are ever in Mexico, you are welcome anytime.

I can't believe that such a wonderful woman chose to marry me. I love you very much and I'm look forward to the years to come.

Best Man

Thanks to Iain, my younger big brother, for being the best man. It was difficult determining whether Iain or Alastair, my twin brother, should be the best man. But I was worried that Elizabeth might get mixed up and marry the wrong person, so I decided Iain might be a safer option.

The stag party was a four-day jaunt to Barcelona and then a four-week period for me to recover. For those of you who know Iain, he's quite into culture and history, so I was looking forward to spending some time visiting monuments and museums, and sampling the local food. Well, the most we saw of Barcelona was a kebab restaurant and bar, which luckily was located right next to our hotel. So, if you're ever in Barcelona and looking for a good kebab, let me know.

Cake / Flowers / Minister / Piper

I'd like to take this opportunity to say a few other thank yous. Firstly, we'd like to thank all of you for your generous gifts and we really appreciate your kindness. Thanks to our minister, Geoff, for conducting the service. I was asking Geoff earlier if he believed in sex before the wedding. And he said, "Not if it delays the ceremony." We would like to thank Hayley Duckworth for the flowers and Jesme Browne for making our wedding cake. We can only imagine the time and effort that went into making it and it looks absolutely delicious and beautiful. So thank you very much.

Ushers

Talking about delicious and beautiful, I would also like to thank our ushers, Alastair, Dan and Paul. Thanks for your work ushering the crowd into the church today. The only specific request we made of the ushers was that they look good. And they let us down somewhat there. But I'm feeling quite honored having Paul here tonight, because it's a Friday night and the Caddy Coy bar is open, as far as I know. But you never know, Paul, you might be able to make the Garage later on. Thanks to all of you today.

Bridesmades

There are three other beautiful ladies here today needing our thanks. Elizabeth's sister Kimberly and close friends Christine and Stacey. We'd like to thank you very much for being such wonderful bridesmaids. You have done a brilliant job helping out with the wedding and making sure Elizabeth didn't run off somewhere at the last minute. Kimberly and Stacey have left their husbands and kids at home in the States, so they're out to party tonight. And well, Christine's always up for a party. All of the bridesmaids are teachers, which is probably a good thing, as I think it takes three teachers to keep Elizabeth in line. We appreciate that you've travelled a long way to be here and thanks again. So, if you would please be up standing and join me in a toast to the bridesmaids. To the bridesmaids.

Printed in Great Britain
by Amazon